Highlights™

LAUGH ATTACK!

The Biggest, Best Joke Book EVER

Highlights Press
Honesdale, Pennsylvania

Contributing Illustrators: David Coulson, Kelly Kennedy, Rich Powell, Kevin Rechin, Pete Whitehead

Published by Highlights for Children
P.O. Box 18201
Columbus, Ohio 43218-0201
Printed in the United States of America

ISBN: 978-1-68437-359-8
First edition

Visit our website at HighlightsPress.com.

10 9 8 7 6 5 4

Contents

An Ocean of Giggles

How do you make a squid laugh?

With ten-tickles.

What kind of fish likes bubble gum?

A blowfish.

How does a fish cut through wood?

It uses a sea saw.

What lives in the sea and carries a lot of people?

An octobus.

What is the best way to catch a fish?

Have someone throw it to you.

What is the most affectionate animal in the sea?

A cuddlefish.

Who eats at underwater restaurants?

Scuba diners.

Why do sea horses only like salt water?

Because pepper water makes them sneeze.

What building is easy to lift?

A lighthouse.

What is an oyster's strongest friend?

A mussel.

What kind of fish goes well with peanut butter?

A jellyfish.

What lives in the ocean and always agrees with you?

A seal of approval.

What is green and has a trunk?

A seasick tourist.

What do you call a clam that doesn't share?

A selfish shellfish.

How much did the crab pay for the sandcastle?

A sand dollar.

Why couldn't Batman and Robin go fishing?

Because Robin kept eating all the worms.

What kind of fish are made for freezing weather?

Skates.

Why couldn't the sailors play cards?

Because the captain was standing on the deck.

What did the sea otter have for lunch?

Abalone sandwich.

What kind of gum do whales chew?

Blubber gum.

Knock, knock.
Who's there?
Walrus.
Walrus who?
Why do you walrus
ask that silly question?

What did the boy octopus say to the girl octopus?

I want to hold your hand, hand, hand, hand, hand, hand, hand, hand.

How do sailors get their clothes clean?

They throw them overboard. Then they are washed ashore.

What do you call two octopuses that look alike?

I-tentacle twins.

Where do sea cows sleep?

In the barn-acle.

What is a knight's favorite food?

Swordfish.

What is stranger than seeing a catfish?

Seeing a goldfish bowl.

What did the beach say when the tide came in?

Long time no sea.

What washes up on tiny beaches?

Microwaves.

How does a mermaid call a friend?

On her shell phone.

What is a shark's favorite game?

Swallow the leader.

What do you get when you cross a school of fish with a herd of elephants?

Swimming trunks.

Why did the sailor sell things on his ship?

It wouldn't go without a sale.

Why do opera singers make good sailors?

They know how to handle high C's.

What is the best way to get around the ocean floor?

Taxi crab.

What do you do with a blue whale?

Cheer it up.

What is a dolphin's favorite TV show?

Whale of Fortune.

Where do crustaceans keep their dishes?

In the crabinets.

Tommy: I went fishing once, and now I can't stop.
Tim: Why? What happened?
Tommy: I got hooked on it.

Game Warden: Didn't you read the sign? It says, "No Fishing."
Ben: I'm not fishing. I'm teaching these worms how to swim.

Why don't fish like to play basketball?

They're afraid of the net.

Why did the fish go to the library?

To find some bookworms.

Why did the dolphin cross the bay?

To get to the other tide.

What does a sea monster eat for dinner?

Fish and ships.

Where do boats go when they are sick?

To the dock.

How did the cod cross the ocean?

Very e-fish-iently.

Seth: Why didn't the octopus want to eat his dinner?

Mark: Because he wasn't hungry?

Seth: No, because he didn't want to wash all of his hands!

Why is the letter *T* like an island?

Because it's in the middle of water.

Tara: Did you give the goldfish fresh water today?

Jackson: No. They didn't finish the water I gave them yesterday.

What does a fish hang on its door at Christmas?

A coral wreath.

Why do sea gulls fly over the sea?

Because if they flew over the bay, they would be bagels.

What did the boy get when he leaned over the back of the boat?

A stern warning.

What is the ocean's best subject?

Current events.

If two fish try out for choir, which one will be chosen?

The one with better scales.

What is the best way to communicate with a fish?

Drop it a line.

Where does bacon go on vacation?

The Pigcific Ocean.

How does a fish feel when it is caught stealing bait?

Gillty.

What vitamin do fish take?

Vitamin sea.

A fisherman carrying a lobster met a friend on the way home. "Where are you going with that lobster under your arm?" asked his friend. The fisherman answered, "I'm taking it home for dinner." Just then, the lobster spoke up. "I've already had my dinner. May we go to a movie instead?"

What is the fastest whale in the world?

Moby Quick!

What do sardines do when they are bored?

Watch telefishion.

What's the difference between a fish and a piano?

You can't tuna fish.

What did one ocean say to the other?

Nothing. It just waved.

What did the mother sardine say to her children when they saw a submarine for the first time?

"Don't be frightened, children—it's only a can of people."

Which game do fish like to play?

Salmon Says.

Tourist: Where is the best place to see a man-eating fish?

Aquarium Guide: At a seafood restaurant.

Comical Cats and Daffy Dogs

What is it called
when a cat wins
a dog show?

A cat-has-trophy.

What do you call a dog magician?

A labracadabrador.

What dog loves to take bubble baths?

A shampoodle.

What do you call an eight-sided cat?

An octopuss.

What kind of dog is like a vampire?

A bloodhound.

What kind of dog can tell time?

A clocker spaniel.

Where should you never take a dog?

A flea market.

What do you call a dog that has the flu?

A germy shepherd.

What dog can play football?

A golden receiver.

Damian: My cat plays chess.

Laurie: Your cat must be really smart!

Damian: Oh, I don't know. I usually beat him two out of three times.

What do you call a cat that drank too much lemonade?

A sourpuss.

Jordan: Do you have any dogs going cheap?

Pet store owner: No, sir. All of our dogs go "Woof."

Kate: Did you like the story about the dog that ran two miles just to pick up a stick?

Nate: No, I thought it was a little farfetched.

What is a dog's favorite book?

Hairy Pawter and the Deathly Howls.

Knock, knock.

Who's there?

Meow.

Meow who?

Take meow to the ball game!

Why did the dog leap for joy?

Joy was holding the cookies.

Where do cats go to look at fine art?

The mewseum.

Why do you have to be careful when it's raining cats and dogs?

So you don't step in a poodle.

What is a dog's favorite movie?

Jurassic Bark.

Ten cats were on a boat. One jumped off. How many were left?

None—they were all copycats.

A woman walked into a pet store and asked,
"Can I get a kitten for my apartment?"
"Sorry," said the store owner, "we don't do trades."

Blake: My dog's the smartest in town. He can say his own name in perfect English.

Allie: What's his name?

Blake: Ruff.

What did the dog say to the car?

"Hey, you're in my barking spot!"

Charlie: What's your dog's name?

Chelsea: Ginger.

Charlie: Does Ginger bite?

Chelsea: No, but Ginger snaps.

Knock, knock.

Who's there?

Detail.

Detail who?

Detail of de cat is on de end.

What's the difference between a comma and a cat?

One means "pause at the end of the clause," and the other means "claws at the end of the paws."

If dogs go to obedience school, where do cats go?

Kittygarten.

What U.S. state do cats and dogs like to visit?

Petsylvania.

What did the cat say when he stubbed his toe?

"Me-ow!"

What did the cat say after she made fun of another cat?

"I'm sorry I hurt your felines. I was just kitten."

How do you get a cat to do tricks?

Put a dog in a catsuit.

Why does a mouse like the letter *S*?

It makes a cat scat.

Knock, knock.

Who's there?

Feline.

Feline who?

I'm feline fine, thanks.

What position does a dog play on the football field?

Rufferee.

What do cats eat for breakfast?

Mice crispies.

What do lazy dogs do?

They chase parked cars.

Knock, knock.
Who's there?
Me.
Me who?
You sure have a funny-sounding cat.

What do you call a cat that goes to the beach on Christmas?

Sandy Claws.

Why can't Dalmatians play hide-and-seek?

They will always be spotted.

What works in the circus, meows, and does somersaults?

An acrocat.

Why did the cat lie on the computer?

To keep an eye on the mouse.

What do invisible cats drink?

Evaporated milk.

When is it bad luck to see a black cat?

When you're a mouse.

What do you call a dog who builds doghouses?

A barkitect.

Knock, knock.
Who's there?
Beagle.
Beagle who?
Beagle with cream cheese.

What kind of dog's favorite subject is science?

A lab.

What do you call it when it rains cats?

A downpurr.

Why did the man take his dog to the railroad station?

To get him trained.

Why did the dog learn to tell time?

Because he wanted to be a watchdog.

How do you identify a dog?

Collar I.D.

Sammy: What kind of dog is that?
Karl: She's a police dog.
Sammy: She doesn't look like a police dog.
Karl: That's because she's undercover.

Tanya: Why is your dog wearing glasses?
Danya: Because contacts bother his eyes.

What magazine do cats like to read?

Good Mousekeeping.

What do you call a dog's kiss?

A pooch smooch.

How does a dog stop a DVD?

He presses the paws button.

Ted: Does your puppy have a license?
Ned: No, he's not old enough to drive.

What does a dog call his father?

Paw.

What do you say to a dog with a sore paw?

"Heal, boy, heal!"

What did the puppy say when he stepped on sandpaper?

"Rough, rough!"

What did the police dog say to the speeder?

"Stop in the name of the paw!"

What do you get if you cross a dog with a frog?

A dog that can lick you from the other side of the road!

Farm Hee-Haws

How does a chicken tell time?

One o'cluck, two o'cluck, three o'cluck . . .

What did the cow say when it had nothing to eat but a thistle?

"Thistle have to do."

How do you keep milk from getting sour?

Leave it in the cow.

Where does a sheep like to stand in line?

At the baaaack.

Why did the sheep jump over the moon?

Because the cow was on vacation.

What kind of jokes do farmers tell?

Corny ones.

What has four legs and flies?

A horse in the summertime.

What does it mean when you find a horseshoe?

Some poor horse is walking around in just his socks.

What kind of machine raises pigs?

A porklift.

What do you call a pig that sat in the sun too long?

Bacon.

How do you fit more pigs on your farm?

Build a styscraper.

What do you put on a bad pig?

Hamcuffs.

Visitor: You sure grow a lot of peaches around here. What do you do with all of them?

Farmer: We eat what we can and can what we can't.

What do you call a teeter-totter for donkeys?

A hee-haw seesaw.

Where do cows go on vacation?

Moo York.

Why do cows wear bells?

Because their horns don't work.

Why did the farmer plant cranberries on the road?

He wanted cranberry juice.

What do you get when you play tug-of-war with a pig?

Pulled pork.

Why is it so hard to talk with a goat?

Because the goat always butts in.

Why do gardeners hate weeds?

If you give them an inch, they'll take a yard.

What happens when a pig loses its voice?

It becomes disgruntled.

Why did the farmer call her pig Ink?

It kept running out of its pen.

Lonnie: Does a cow remind you of something?
Jennie: No, but it does ring a bell.

What animal always sleeps with its shoes on?

A horse.

What does a cow use to cut grass?

A lawnmooer.

What do you call a line of rabbits walking backward?

A receding hare line.

What has four legs and says, "Oom, oom"?

A cow walking backwards.

What has twelve tails, one horn, and squeals?

A dozen pigs in a truck.

What do flowers say when they explode?

"Ka-bloooom!"

What did the apple tree say to the farmer?

"Quit picking on me."

How do you make a milkshake?

Give a cow a pogo stick.

How do you make a turkey float?

With two scoops of ice cream, a bottle of root beer, and a turkey.

What did the mare say when she finished
her hay?

"That's the last straw."

Noelle: Where does a donkey go on a field trip?
Peter: I don't know. Where?
Noelle: To a mule-seum!

What wakes up a rooster?

An alarm clock-a-doodle-doo.

Farmer: Hey there! What are you doing up in
my tree?
Sam: Just obeying your sign. The one that says
KEEP OFF THE GRASS.

You throw away the outside, cook the inside, eat the
outside, and throw away the inside. What is it?

An ear of corn.

When is a dog's tail like a farmer's cart?

When it's a-waggin' (wagon).

Why did the farmer throw vegetables on the ground?

He wanted peas on Earth.

How do you mend a berry bush?

With a strawberry patch.

What was the worm doing in the cornfield?

Going in one ear and out the other.

What do you call a sleeping bull?

A bulldozer.

What does a farmer do when his sheep are hurt?

He calls a lambulance.

What do you call a royal horse?

His Majesteed.

What do horses put on their burgers?

Mayo-neighs.

Why did the sheep keep going straight down the street?

No ewe turns were allowed.

What do horses do at bedtime?

They hit the hay.

What do you call the father of an ear of corn?

Popcorn.

What kind of pictures do sheep paint?

Lambscapes.

Why did the farmer plant money in her garden?

She wanted rich soil.

Agriculture Student: I'd be surprised if you got ten pounds of apples from that tree.
Farmer: So would I. It's a pear tree.

What kind of vegetables do you pick in the winter?

Snow peas.

What is the definition of a farmer?

Someone who is outstanding in his field.

Where do sheep go to get their hair cut?

The baa baa shop.

How did the farmer fix his jeans?

With a cabbage patch.

Why did the pig want to be an actor?

He was a big ham.

How did the farmer find his daughter when she was lost?

He tractor.

What happened when the pigpen broke?

The pig used a pencil.

Where did the first corn come from?

The stalk brought it.

Impatient Gardener: This whole row of seeds hasn't sprouted yet!

Patient Gardener: Don't worry. They'll turnip.

Farm Helper: Can you tell me how long cows should be milked?

Farmer: They should be milked the same as short cows.

What is a cow's favorite movie?

The Sound of Moosic.

THIS IS A LEG.

How many legs does a horse have if you call its tail a leg?

Four. Calling its tail a leg doesn't make it one!

Why can't you tell a secret in a cornfield?

There are too many ears.

Tina: I just heard that Chuck bought a farm a mile long and an inch wide.
Sam: Really? What could he grow on a farm that size?
Tina: Spaghetti.

Knock, knock.
Who's there?
Goat.
Goat who?
Goat to the door and find out.

What do you call potatoes that ripen at the end of the season?

Later taters.

What do you get when you cross potato plants with squash plants?

Mashed potatoes.

What did the plant say to the gardener?

Take me to your weeder.

What are the most difficult beans to grow?

Jelly beans.

Wacky Wildlife

What do you call a lost wolf?

A where-wolf.

What do you get when you cross a porcupine and a turtle?

A slowpoke.

What is a skunk's favorite sandwich?

Peanut butter and smelly.

What does a snail riding on a turtle's back say?

"Woo hoo!"

What did the judge say when the skunk walked into the courtroom?

"Odor in the court!"

How much money does a skunk have?

One scent.

Mother Mouse was taking her children for a stroll. Suddenly a large cat appeared in their path. Mother Mouse shouted "Bow-wow-wow!" and the cat scurried away. "You see, my children," Mother Mouse said, "it pays to learn a second language."

Ron: What kind of sandwiches do bears like?
John: I don't know. What kind?
Ron: Growled-cheese sandwiches.

Audrey: My pet turtle turned two today!
Tara: Cool! Are you going to shellebrate his birthday?

Where do rabbits go after their wedding?

On their bunnymoon.

Who did the baby deer invite to her birthday party?

Her nearest and deer-est friends.

What do funny frogs sit on?

Silly pads.

Trinity: What do you get when you cross a bear and a skunk?

Kristy: I don't know. What?

Trinity: I don't know either, but it can easily get a seat on the bus!

What did the porcupine say to the cactus?

"Are you my mother?"

What do you get when you cross a science-fiction film with a toad?

Star Warts.

What do you get when you cross a bear with a rain cloud?

A drizzly bear.

What do you call a rabbit who is angry in the summertime?

A hot, cross bunny.

What is a female deer's favorite ice-cream flavor?

Cookie doe.

What animal likes letters?

An alpha-bat.

How do you know carrots are good for your eyes?

You never see rabbits wearing glasses.

What do you get when you cross Bambi with a ghost?

Bamboo.

What is a bunny's favorite kind of music?

Hip-hop.

Knock, knock.
Who's there?
Moose.
Moose who?
Moose you be so nosy?

Knock, knock.
Who's there?
Weasel.
Weasel who?
Weasel while you work.

Nora: Why do bears paint their faces yellow?

Flora: I don't know. Why?

Nora: So they can hide in banana trees.

Flora: Impossible! I've never seen a bear in a banana tree.

Nora: See? It works!

Knock, knock.

Who's there?

Grrr.

Grrr who?

Are you a bear or an owl?

What game do mice play?

Hide-and-squeak.

What mouse was a Roman emperor?

Julius Cheeser.

What do you call a bear with no fur?

A bare bear.

Why did Sally bring her skunk to school?

For show-and-smell.

Where do bunnies live?

In a rabbitat.

What do you get if you cross a rabbit with fleas?

A bugs bunny.

What did the otter say to the superstar?

"Can I have your otter-graph?"

What kind of snake keeps its car the cleanest?

A windshield viper.

One day a bat left to get food and returned with a huge bump on his head.

First bat: What happened?

Second bat: You see that tree over there?

First bat: Yes.

Second bat: Well, I didn't.

What do rabbits use to measure diamonds?

Carrots (carats).

Doctor: What brings you to my office today?
Squirrel: I just realized that I am what I eat. Nuts!

Knock, knock.
Who's there?
Beaver E.
Beaver E who?
Beaver E quiet and nobody will hear us.

What is a rabbit's favorite candy?

Lolli-hops.

What kind of party do mice throw when they move into a new home?

A mouse-warming party.

How many skunks does it take to make a big stink?

A phew.

Knock, knock.
Who's there?
Panther.
Panther who?
Panther what I wear on my legths.

What do you call a flying skunk?

A smelly-copter.

What is a mole's favorite book?

The digtionary.

What did the beaver say to the tree?

"It was nice gnawing (knowing) you."

Why didn't the cub leave his mommy?

He couldn't bear it!

How do you know that carrots are good for your eyes?

Have you ever seen a rabbit wearing glasses?

Bug Belly Laughs

How do slugs begin fairy tales?

"Once upon a slime . . ."

What did the bee say when it returned to the hive?

"Honey, I'm home!"

What kind of bug tells time?

A clockroach.

First firefly: You've gotten taller since I last saw you.
Second firefly: I guess I'm having a glow spurt!

What did one flea say to the other flea?

"Should we walk or take the dog?"

What did one worm say to the other worm?

"Where in earth have you been?"

What do you call a party for fleas?

A flea-esta.

What do you call a nervous cricket?

A jitterbug.

What are caterpillars afraid of?

Dog-erpillars.

Passenger on plane: Those people down there look like ants!
Flight attendant: They are ants. We haven't left the ground yet.

Knock, knock.
Who's there?
Gnats.
Gnats who?
Gnats not a bit funny.

What did one girl firefly say to the other girl firefly?

"You glow, girl!"

Which type of bee is hard to understand?

A mumblebee.

Knock, knock.
Who's there?
Weevil.
Weevil who?
Weevil stay only a few minutes.

What kind of bee trips over its own feet?

A stumblebee.

What do you call a fly with a damaged wing?

A walk.

What kind of insect can you wear?

A yellow jacket.

What do you call a traveling flea?

An itch-hiker.

What does every tarantula wish he had?

A hairy godmother.

What is a spider's favorite picnic food?

Corn on the cobweb.

What's worse than finding a worm in your apple?

Finding half a worm in your apple.

How do bees get to school?

They take the school buzz.

What kind of insects are bad at football?

Fumblebees.

What happened to the two bed bugs who met in the mattress?

They got married in the spring.

What did the spider do when he got a new car?

He took it out for a spin.

What do you get if you cross a tarantula with a rose?

I'm not sure, but I wouldn't try smelling it!

How does a caterpillar start his day?

He turns over a new leaf.

How do you find out where a flea has bitten you?

Start from scratch.

Why don't fleas catch cold?

They're always in fur coats.

What goes zzub, zzub?

A bee flying backwards.

What do you call a musical insect?

A humbug.

Why do bees hum?

Because they don't know the words.

What is a bumblebee's least favorite musical note?

Bee flat!

Why do bees itch?

Because they have hives.

What do you call a ladybug's husband?

Lord Bug.

How do fireflies start a race?

"Ready, Set, Glow!"

How do you know which end of a worm is its head?

Tickle the middle and see which end laughs.

Where do bees go when they get hurt?

To the waspital.

What is smarter than a talking bird?

A spelling bee.

Amelia: What has nine legs, twenty eyes, and pink fur?

Matt: I don't know.

Amelia: I don't know either, but it's crawling on your shoulder!

Camp Counselor: How did you get that horrible swelling on your nose?

Jimmy: I bent down to smell a brose.

Camp Counselor: There's no b in rose.

Jimmy: There was in this one!

How do spiders learn definitions?

They use the Web-ster's Dictionary.

Why do bees have sticky hair?

Because they use honeycombs.

Knock, knock.
Who's there?
Beehive.
Beehive who?
Beehive yourself or else.

Why did the lady who swallowed a fly have to miss work?

She had a stomach bug.

Knock, knock.
Who's there?
Flea.
Flea who?
Flea blind mice.

Why did the spider leave home?

It wanted to change websites.

What vegetable do bugs hate?

Squash.

Knock, knock.

Who's there?

Roach.

Roach who?

I roach you a letter—did you get it?

If a moth breathes oxygen in sunlight, what does it breathe in the dark?

Nightrogen.

Knock, knock.

Who's there?

Spider.

Spider who?

In spider everything, I still like you.

How do fleas travel from place to place?

By itch-hiking.

What's the best way to prevent infection from biting insects?

Don't bite them.

What do you get when you cross a chicken and a centipede?

Enough drumsticks to feed an army!

What do you call two spiders that just got married?

Newlywebs.

Why was the mother firefly unhappy?

Because her children weren't that bright.

What do you get when you cross a sheep and a honeybee?

Bah humbug!

Why didn't the butterfly go to the dance?

Because it was a mothball.

Two flies are on the porch. Which one is the actor?

The one on the screen.

What is the definition of slug?

A snail with a housing problem.

What do you call an undercover arachnid?

A spy-der.

Funny Food

How do clowns like their eggs?

Funny-side up.

What do bakers put on their beds?

Cookie sheets.

What do you get if you eat pasta while you're sick?

Macaroni and sneeze.

Why did the banana go to the doctor?

Because it wasn't peeling well.

Why can't you feed a teddy bear?

Because it's already stuffed.

What did the ham do when he wanted to talk to the salami?

He called a meat-ing.

What do you call a shivering glass of milk?

A milkshake.

Knock, knock.
Who's there?
Pickle.
Pickle who?
Pickle little flower to give to your mother.

How did the egg cross the frying pan?

It scrambled.

What do you get when you cross a watermelon with a bus?

A fruit that can seat forty-five people.

Where do hamburgers dance?

At a meatball.

How do you make a strawberry shake?

By taking it to a scary movie.

Knock, knock.
Who's there?
Paris.
Paris who?
A Paris good, but I'd rather have an orange.

Why couldn't the egg lend his friend money?

Because he was broke.

Knock, knock.

Who's there?

Banana.

Banana who?

Knock, knock.

Who's there?

Banana.

Banana who?

Knock, knock.

Who's there?

Orange.

Orange who?

Orange you glad I didn't say banana?

Why should you knock before you open the refrigerator?

You might see the salad dressing.

What does a sweet potato wear to bed?

Its yammies.

Why is bread lots of fun?

It's made of wheeeat.

What do you give to a puppy that has a fever?

Mustard—it's the best thing for a hot dog.

Knock, knock.
Who's there?
Pudding.
Pudding who?
Pudding on your shoes before your pants is a bad idea.

What side dish do miners eat?

Coal slaw.

What is a boxer's favorite drink?

Fruit punch.

In mathematics, what is the law of the doughnut?

Two halves make a hole.

What do you get if you eat uranium?

Atomic ache.

What starts with T, ends with T, and is full of T?

A teapot.

Why were U, V, W, X, Y, and Z late to the tea party?

Because they always come after T.

What did the pepperoni say when it needed to take notes?

"May I have a pizza paper and a pen?"

How do you make a hot dog stand?

Take away its chair.

Knock, knock,
Who's there?
Handsome.
Handsome who?
Handsome of those cookies over,
please. I'm hungry!

Knock, knock.
Who's there?
Doughnut.
Doughnut who?
Doughnut open this until your birthday.

What is the most adorable vegetable?

The cutecumber.

Why didn't the hot dog star in the movies?

The rolls weren't good enough.

How do you fix a broken pizza?

With tomato paste.

How do you turn soup into gold?

Add twenty-four carrots.

How do you make an egg roll?

Push it.

What did the green grape say to the purple grape?

"Breathe!"

Knock, knock.
Who's there?
Honeycomb.
Honeycomb who?
Honeycomb your hair—it's tangled.

What do you get when you cross a banana with a knife?

A banana split.

What do you call a banana with wings?

A fruit fly.

When's the best time to eat a banana?

After it's peeled.

How do you make a cream puff?

Take it jogging.

Why did the cookie cry?

His mom had been a wafer so long.

Why was the little apple so excited?

He was going to see his Granny Smith.

What did one tray say to the other?

"Lunch is on me today!"

What did the hamburger name its daughter?

Patty.

What do chess players have for breakfast?

Pawncakes.

Knock, knock.
Who's there?
Ice-cream soda.
Ice-cream soda who?
**Ice-cream soda whole world will know
how silly I am!**

How do you make hot dogs shiver?

Put chili beans on them.

Why did the orange use sunblock?

Because it was starting to peel.

What is the laziest food ever?

Bread—it just loafs around.

What is a camera's favorite kind of sandwich?

Cheese.

What do you get if you drop a basket of fruit?

Fruit salad.

Danny: Waiter, this soup tastes funny.

Waiter: Then why aren't you laughing?

Diner: What is this fly doing in my soup?

Waiter: It looks like it's doing the backstroke.

Diner: There's a fly in my soup!

Waiter: Don't worry. The spider on the bread will take care of it.

What do you call a person who serves you meals in the water?

A wader.

Diner: Look at this chicken. One leg is longer than the other!

Waitress: Are you going to eat it or dance with it?

Diner: Waiter, I'm in a hurry. Will the pancakes be long?

Waiter: No, they'll be round.

What did one potato chip say to the other potato chip?

"Want to go for a dip?"

What did the butter say to the brake?

"Why did you stop? I was on a roll."

Who are the police of the fruit world?

The apri-cops.

Where are French fries born?

In Greece.

Why did the orange stop in the middle of the road?

It ran out of juice.

What do you say when someone wants your cheese?

Sorry, but that's nacho cheese.

Who is the leader of the popcorn?

The kernel.

Knock, knock.
Who's there?
Carrot.
Carrot who?
Don't you carrot all about me?

What is green and goes "slam, slam, slam, slam"?
A four-door pickle.

What do beavers eat for breakfast?

Oakmeal.

What is the best time to eat a banana?

When the moment is ripe.

What did the hot dog say when it finished the race first?

"I'm the wiener!"

Tomato: I had a nightmare last night. I dreamed I was a salad.

Broccoli: What's so bad about that?

Tomato: I tossed all night!

What is the best thing to put in a pie?

Your teeth.

Knock, knock.

Who's there?

Muffin.

Muffin who?

There's muffin the matter with me—I'm doing fine!

What did the hairdresser say to the hot dog?

Let's put you in a bun.

What did the nut say when it sneezed?

"Cashew!"

What does a cookie say when it's excited?

"Chip, chip, hooray!"

Pig: Why are you eating alphabet soup?

Cow: Because if I were eating number soup, I'd be a cowculator!

Rosey: Which do you like better, salt or pepper?

Stephanie: Pepper.

Rosey: What? How insalting!

What do you call rotten eggs, rotten fruit, and spoiled milk in a bag?

Grosseries.

Knock, knock.
Who's there?
Candy.
Candy who?
Candy cow jump over the moon?

Knock, knock,
Who's there?
Omelet.
Omelet who?
Omelet smarter than you think.

What dip do bathtubs eat at parties?

Shower cream and onion.

What is a tortilla chip's favorite kind of dance?

Salsa.

What is a tree's favorite drink?

Root beer.

Knock, knock.
Who's there?
Turnip.
Turnip who?
Turnip the heat—it's cold in here.

What did the cook name his son?

Stew.

What did the syrup say to its long-lost friend?

"It's been a waffle long time!"

What did the ear of corn say when it was about to be peeled?

"Shucks."

Stella: So you're going to start a bakery?
Heidi: Yes, if I can raise the dough.

Jim: There are only two things I can't eat for breakfast.

Kelly: Really? What are they?

Jim: Lunch and dinner.

Joseph: Every day my uncle goes into the kitchen, and every day he cooks something different. Do you know what he always makes?

Lisa: You just said he cooks something different every day.

Joseph: Yes, but he always makes a mess.

Why did the bacon laugh?

Because the egg cracked a yolk.

Knock, knock.
Who's there?
Dishes.
Dishes who?
Dishes me. Can I come in?

Sue: What are we having for dinner?

Jim: Oh, hundreds of things.

Sue: Good! What are they?

Jim: Beans!

Diner: Waiter, there's no chicken in my chicken potpie!

Waiter: Would you expect to find a dog in a dog biscuit, sir?

Why don't bananas snore?

Because they don't want to wake the rest of the bunch.

Knock, knock.

Who's there?

Barbie.

Barbie who?

Barbie Q.

How did the calendar survive on a desert island?

It ate the dates.

What does a frog order at a restaurant?

French flies and a cherry croak.

What is a volcano's favorite food?

Magma-roni and cheese.

Why did the baker stop making doughnuts?

He got tired of the hole business.

Knock, knock.
Who's there?
Apple.
Apple who?
Apple on the door, but it doesn't open.

Knock, knock.
Who's there?
Bacon.
Bacon who?
I'm bacon a cake for your birthday.

Knock, knock.
Who's there?
Butter.
Butter who?
Butter bring an umbrella—it looks like rain.

Knock, knock.
Who's there?
Fajita.
Fajita who?
Fajita another thing, I'll be stuffed.

Knock, knock.
Who's there?
Stew.
Stew who?
Stew early to go to bed.

David: Do we have any tomato paste, Mom?
Mom: Why do you need it
David: I just broke a tomato.

Diner: Waiter, there is a bee in my alphabet soup!
Waiter: Yes, sir. I'm sure there is an A, a C, and all the other letters, too.

Diner: Do you serve crabs?
Waiter: Yes, we serve anyone.

What is the loudest kind of sports equipment?

A racket.

Sports Bloopers

What baseball team does a jokester like best?

The New York Prankees.

What do championship football players eat their cereal in?

Super bowls.

What is a basketball player's favorite cheese?

Swish.

Why did the ballerina quit?

Because it was tutu hard.

Why couldn't the chicken get on base?

Because she kept hitting fowl balls.

What did the umpire say to the car?

"Steer-ike one!"

What do you call a pig that plays basketball?

A ball hog.

What do you call a pig that knows karate?

A pork chop.

What is a pig's favorite position in baseball?

Snortstop.

What did the glove say to the baseball?

"Catch you later!"

Why do porcupines never lose games?

Because they always have the most points.

What did one golfer say to the other?

"May the course be with you."

What can you serve but not eat?

A tennis ball.

What do you call a fly with no wings?

A walk.

Why was the piano tuner hired to play on the baseball team?

Because he had perfect pitch.

What animal is best at hitting a baseball?

A bat.

How does a sneaker sneeze?

"A tennis shoe! A tennis shoe!"

Why did Tarzan spend so much time on the golf course?

He was perfecting his swing.

Why did the golfer wear two pairs of pants?

In case he got a hole in one.

What do you get if you cross a dinosaur and a football player?

A quarterback no one can tackle.

What do hockey players and magicians have in common?

Both do hat tricks.

Why did the basketball player go to jail?

Because he shot the ball.

What is the quietest game in the world?

Bowling—you can hear a pin drop.

Anna: Where are you taking that skunk?
Danny: To the gym.
Anna: What about the smell?
Danny: Oh, he'll get used to it.

What is an insect's favorite sport?

Cricket.

What is the first thing a ball does when it stops rolling?

It looks round.

What did the King of Hearts say to the King of Spades?

"Let's make a deal."

What did the cat say when it struck out at the baseball game?

"Me-out."

What's harder to catch the faster you run?

Your breath.

Why do frogs make good outfielders?

Because they never miss a fly.

What do you call four bullfighters in quicksand?

Cuatro sinko.

What is a hand's favorite sport?

Finger skating.

What is a snowman's favorite game?

Freezebee.

What is a ghost's favorite position in soccer?

Ghoulkeeper.

What has four legs and catches flies?

Two outfielders.

What do you do if the basketball court gets flooded?

Call in the subs.

When is a baby good at basketball?

When it's dribbling.

When do basketball players love doughnuts?

When they dunk them.

What is a cheerleader's favorite color?

Yeller.

Why did the baseball player leave in the middle of his game?

Because his coach told him to run home.

Why do tires get upset when they go bowling?

Because they never make strikes, just spares.

Kelly: How was your roller-skating lesson?
Michael: OK, I guess.
Kelly: What was the hardest part?
Michael: The pavement.

If your watch is broken, why can't you play sports?

Because you don't have the time.

Why is a basketball game equal to a dollar?

Both are made up of four quarters.

What time of year is it best to use a trampoline?

In the springtime.

In what sport do you sit down going up and stand up going down?

Skiing.

Why don't golfers usually drink coffee?

They always carry tees.

What should you drink when you're watching your favorite sports game?

Root beer.

Fran: I sure liked my first football game.

Dan: I did, too, but what was all the fuss about twenty-five cents?

Fran: What do you mean?

Dan: Well, every time somebody caught the ball, the people yelled, "Get the quarterback! Get the quarterback!"

Why was the man doing the backstroke?

He didn't want to swim on a full stomach.

Why did the football coach go to the bank?

He wanted his quarterback.

What type of drink do football players hate?

Penaltea.

Why did the football coach send in his second string?

To tie up the game.

What do you call a spoiled tightrope walker?

An acrobrat.

What flavor of ice cream do bikers like the least?

Rocky road.

Why is Cinderella bad at basketball?

Because she runs away from the ball.

What's a golfer's favorite letter?

T.

What is a waiter's favorite sport?

Tennis, because he serves so well.

What is the hardest part about skydiving?

The ground.

What has 18 legs and catches flies?

A baseball team.

What's the best part of a boxer's joke?

The punch line.

How do basketball players stay cool during the game?

They stand close to the fans.

Why was the baseball player invited to go on the camping trip?

To pitch the tent.

Why did the baseball bat go to the recording studio?

To get a big hit.

Which baseball team do puppies play for?

The New York Pets.

What do baseball and pancakes have in common?

They both need the batter.

Spooky Sillies

What is a vampire's favorite animal?

A giraffe.

What does a vampire stand on after taking a shower?

A bat mat.

What do you call a skeleton that is always telling lies?

A bony phony.

What do you get if you cross a witch and an iceberg?

A cold spell.

What do you call a wizard from outer space?

A flying sorcerer.

What do you call a pumpkin that thinks it's a comedian?

A joke-o'-lantern.

Which kind of ghost haunts a chicken coop?

A poultrygeist.

What do you call a skeleton snake?

A rattler.

What do you call a prehistoric ghost?

A terrordactyl.

Knock, knock.
Who's there?
Boo.
Boo who?
Don't be scared—it's only a joke.

What do you call a clean, neat, hardworking, kind, intelligent monster?

A failure.

What's white, black, and blue all over?

A ghost that can't go through walls.

Who is the smartest monster?

Frank Einstein.

Why did the monster need braces?

Because he had an ogre-bite.

What do you call two witches who share an apartment?

Broommates.

What did one zombie say to the other?

"Get a life."

Who won the monster beauty contest?

Nobody.

How do you make a witch itch?

Take away the W.

What do you do with a green monster?

Wait until it ripens.

Why is Halloween so fun for ghouls?

Because Halloween is a ghoul's best friend.

Knock, knock.
Who's there?
Goblin.
Goblin who?
Goblin your food will give you a tummyache.

Why did the vampire keep falling for the oldest tricks in the book?

Because he's a sucker.

Why did the Cyclops stop teaching?

Because he had only one pupil.

Why are skeletons so calm, cool, and collected?

Because nothing gets under their skin.

What do monsters put on before they go in the pool?

Sunscream.

Knock, knock.

Who's there?

Howl.

Howl who?

Howl you know unless you open the door?

Who is the best dancer at a Halloween party?

The boogieman.

Where do ghosts go for a vacation?

The Boohamas.

What's a vampire's favorite dance?

The fangdango.

How do witches tell time?

By looking at their witchwatches.

What is a vampire's favorite holiday?

Fangsgiving.

What is a goblin's favorite ride at the amusement park?

The roller ghoster.

Who turns off the lights on Halloween?

The light's witch.

Where do witches get their hair done?

The ugly parlor.

Why don't skeletons work as stunt men?

They don't have the guts.

What do ghosts do at garage sales?

They go bargain haunting.

Why don't skeletons play music in church?

They have no organs.

What do witches love about their computers?

The spell checker.

Why did the ghost get kicked out of the football game?

Because he screamed, "Boo!"

How do monsters tell their futures?

They read their horrorscopes.

Why do ghosts make good cheerleaders?

Because they have a lot of spirit.

Why don't vampires have any friends?

Because they're a pain in the neck.

What is a ghost's favorite sandwich?

Booloney.

What do baby ghosts wear on their feet?

Booties.

What does a witch request at a hotel?

Broom service.

How do skeletons get their mail?

By bony express.

What is a ghost's favorite day of the week?

Frightday.

What is Dracula's favorite type of coffee?

Decoffinated.

What would you get if you crossed a snowball with a vampire?

Frostbite.

What do you call a giant mummy?

Gauzilla.

What do ghosts eat for dinner?

Ghoulash.

Why did the boy carry a clock and a bird on Halloween?

He was going tick-or-tweeting.

What does a ghost put on its bagel?

Scream cheese.

Which three letters would surprise the Invisible Man?

I-C-U.

CRUSH! SMASH! CRUNCH!

First giant monster: We must be getting close to a city.
Second giant monster: How can you tell?
First giant monster: We're stepping on more cars.

What do vampires put on their holiday turkey?

Gravey.

Knock, knock.
Who's there?
Fangs.
Fangs who?
Fangs for letting me in.

What do ghosts eat for breakfast?
Scream of wheat.

Why did the witch put her broom in the washing machine?
She wanted a clean sweep.

What do ghosts have in the seats of their cars?
Sheet belts.

What sound does a witch's cereal make?
Snap, cackle, and pop.

What is a witch's favorite subject?
Spelling.

Knock, knock.
Who's there?
Thumping.
Thumping who?
Thumping green and thlimy is crawling up your leg.

Knock, knock.
Who's there?
Zombies.
Zombies who?
Only zombies in hives make honey.

What do you call a witch who likes the beach
but is scared of the water?

A chicken sandwitch.

What kind of horse does the boogeyman ride?

A nightmare.

What is a skeleton's favorite instrument?

A trombone.

What goes "cackle, cackle, bonk"?

A witch laughing her head off.

Where's the best place to build a haunted house?

A dead-end street.

Why didn't the witch sing at the concert?

Because she had a frog in her throat.

Why did Frankenstein's monster like the stand-up comic?

Because she kept him in stitches.

Why did the vampire give up acting?

He couldn't sink his teeth into the part.

Why did Dracula go to the doctor?

He was coffin.

What happened when the werewolf swallowed a clock?

He got ticks.

What do Hawaiian ghosts say?

"Happy Hulaween!"

Why did the skeleton go to the barbecue pit?

To get a sparerib.

What kind of jewels do ghosts wear?

Tombstones.

What do you call a ghost's mother and father?

Transparents.

What do you get if you cross a dinosaur with a wizard?

Tyrannosaurus hex.

Knock, knock.
Who's there?
Vampire.
Vampire who?
The Vampire State Building.

What's the only music a Halloween mummy listens to?

Wrap.

Knock, knock.
Who's there?
Gargoyle.
Gargoyle who?
If you gargoyle with salt water, your throat will feel better.

What did one ghost say to the other ghost?

"Do you believe in people?"

What did the people say when the goo monsters attacked?

"Ooze going to save us?"

What did the wizard say to his girlfriend?

"You look wanderful tonight."

What's the best way to talk to a monster?

Long distance.

What is a ghoul's favorite cheese?

Monsterella.

When do Halloween monsters eat their candy?

On Chewsday.

What is the difference between a witch and the letters M-A-K-E-S?

One makes spells and the others spell makes.

Why didn't the zombie go to school?

He felt rotten.

Why didn't the skeleton like recess?

He had no body to play with.

How do you greet a French skeleton?

"Bonejour."

Ted: I didn't know our school was haunted.

Ned: Neither did I. How did you find out?

Ted: Everybody's been talking about our school spirit!

Where do you find the most famous dragons?

In the Hall of Flame.

Knock, knock.
Who's there?
Witches.
Witches who?
Witches the way to go home?

What kind of tests do they give in witch school?
Hexaminations.

What kind of writing does a witch use?
Curse-ive.

What's the best game to play at Halloween?
Hide-and-shriek.

How many witches does it take to change a light bulb?
Just one, but she changes it into a toad.

High-Flying Funnies

How do baby birds learn to fly?

They just wing it.

Knock, knock.
Who's there?
Who.
Who who?
I didn't know you spoke Owl!

What do you get if you cross a bird, a car, and a dog?
A flying carpet.

Why are pigeons so good at baseball?
Because they always know how to get home.

What is the difference between a fly and a bird?
A bird can fly, but a fly can't bird!

What do you call a crate full of ducks?
A box of quackers.

Jennifer: Do you want to hear a bird joke?
Jade: No, thanks.
Jennifer: Well, this is "hawk"ward . . .

Why does a flamingo stand on one leg?

If it lifted both legs, it would fall over!

Jake: What do most birds have?
Torey: Wings.
Jake: Can you repeat that?
Torey: Wing! Wing! Wing!
Jake: Hello? Hello?

James: What did the crow say to the robber?
Kim: I don't know. What?
James: "Stop in the name of the caw!"

Tallulah: Turkey, what are you thankful for?
Turkey: Tofu!

What's black and white and red all over?

A sunburned penguin.

What is black and white and blue all over?

A shivering penguin.

Ozzie: How much birdseed should I buy?
Store Clerk: How many birds do you have?
Ozzie: None, but I want to grow some.

Knock, knock.
Who's there?
Baby owl.
Baby owl who?
Baby owl see you later.

What do you call a bird that stays up north during winter?

A brrrrrd.

What bird can lift the most weight?

A crane.

What's noisier than a whooping crane?

A trumpeting swan.

Knock, knock.
Who's there?
Stork.
Stork who?
Better stork up on food before the storm.

Marielle: I know someone who thinks he's an owl.
Brett: Who?
Marielle: Make that two people.

What do you get when you cross a caterpillar and a parrot?

A walkie talkie.

What do you call a hawk that can draw and play guitar?

Talonted.

Where do birds stay when they're on vacation?

At a cheep hotel.

What time did the duck wake up this morning?

At the quack of dawn.

What do you call a bird that smells bad?

A foul fowl.

What is the rudest bird?

A mockingbird.

If you crossed a snake with a robin, what kind of bird would you get?

A swallow.

Why did the sea gull fly over the sea?

Because if he flew over the bay, he'd be a bagel.

Why do birds fly south for the winter?

Because it's too far to walk.

Why do pelicans carry fish in their beaks?

Because they haven't got any pockets.

What animal has fangs and webbed feet?

Count Duckula.

What bird never goes to the barber?

A bald eagle.

What do mallards wear to fancy events?

Ducksedos.

What is a bird's favorite game?

Fly-and-seek.

How did the bird get to the doctor's office?

He flu.

What did the duck do after the goose told him a joke?

He quacked up.

How is a penny like a turkey sitting on a fence?

Head's on one side, tail's on the other.

Knock, knock.
Who's there?
Ostrich.
Ostrich who?
**Ostrich my arms
up to the sky.**

**What is a bird's
favorite drink?**

Hot cuckoo.

What is the saddest bird?

The blue jay.

Who stole the soap from the bathtub?

The robber ducky.

How do birds fly in the rain?

They use their wing-shield wipers.

What was the goal of the detective duck?

To quack the case.

What did the veterinarian give the sick bird?

Tweetment.

What song do penguins sing on a birthday?

"Freeze a Jolly Good Fellow."

What sound does a hummingbird make while she's thinking?

"Hmmm."

Knock, knock.
Who's there?
Toucan.
Toucan who?
Toucan play this game.

Customer: How much is that bird?

Clerk: Ten dollars, ma'am.

Customer: I'll take it. Will you send me the bill?

Clerk: I'm sorry, ma'am. You'll have to take the whole bird.

What bird is always out of breath?

A puffin.

How do monkeys get downstairs?

They slide down the bananaster.

How do monkeys stay in shape?

They go to the jungle gym.

What did the gorilla eat before dinner?

An ape-etizer.

Delia: What do you call a gorilla wearing earmuffs?
Doug: I don't know. What?
Delia: It doesn't matter. He can't hear you.

Why did the lemur cross the road?

He had to take care of some monkey business.

Why did the monkey eat so many bananas?

He liked them a bunch.

What did the gorilla call his wife?

His prime mate.

What is a chimpanzee's favorite flavor of ice cream?

Mint-chocolate chimp.

What is a monkey's favorite dessert?

Meringue-utan.

What do you call a monkey that eats a lot of potato chips?

A chipmunk.

What do you call a restaurant that throws food in your face?

A monkey business.

What do you call a monkey with all his bananas taken away?

Furious George.

Zane: I heard they taught monkeys to fly.

Kelly: You're kidding!

Zane: Nope. They're called hot-air baboons!

Knock, knock.

Who's there?

Monkey.

Monkey who?

Monkey won't fit. That's why I knocked!

What do you call an exploding monkey?

A ba-boom.

What is the first thing a monkey learns in school?

His ape, B, C's.

Julie: What's the difference between a chimpanzee and a carton of milk?
Ryan: I don't know. What?
Julie: Remind me not to send you to the grocery store!

What kind of key opens a banana?

A monkey.

Who was the chimp's favorite American president?

Ape-raham Lincoln.

What side of a monkey has the most fur?

The outside.

Why did King Kong climb the Empire State Building?

Because he couldn't fit in the elevator.

Why did the gorilla like the banana?

Because it had appeal.

What do you get when King Kong walks through your vegetable garden?

Squash.

Why can't you take a picture of a monkey with a hat?

Because you can't take a picture with a hat!

Gorilla keeper: My gorilla is sick. Do you know a good animal doctor?

Zookeeper: No, I'm afraid all the doctors I know are people.

Why doesn't the elephant use the computer?

It's afraid of the mouse.

Why don't cheetahs ever take baths?

Because they don't want to be spotless.

What wears glass slippers and weighs ten thousand pounds?

Cinderellephant.

What's the best thing to do if an elephant sneezes?

Get out of its way!

Why do giraffes have long necks?

Because their feet smell.

What do you get when you cross a cheetah and a sheep?

A polka-dotted sweater.

What's black and white and red all over?

A zebra with a sunburn.

What is black and white and blue?

A zebra with a cold.

Knock, knock.
Who's there?
Safari.
Safari who?
Safari so good!

What does a hippo get if he stops shaving?

A hippopatamustache.

What's as big as an elephant but weighs nothing?

An elephant's shadow.

Knock, knock.
Who's there?
Hippo.
Hippo who?
Hippo birthday to you!

Knock, knock.
Who's there?
Giraffe.
Giraffe who?
Giraffe anything to eat? I'm hungry!

Where can you win the world's tallest animal?
At a gi-raffle.

Why is a leopard bad at hiding?
Because it's always spotted.

What is a leopard's favorite day?
Chewsday.

Why did the old hippo go to the hospital?

He needed a hippoperation.

How does a lion paddle a canoe?

It uses its roar.

What do you get when two giraffes collide?

A giraffic jam.

What would you do if an elephant sat in front of you at a movie?

Miss most of the film.

How can you tell a water buffalo from a mouse?

Try to pick it up. If you can't, it's a water buffalo.

Why are elephants so wrinkled?

Well, did you ever try to iron one?

What are old bowling balls used as?

Marbles for elephants.

When do giraffes have eight legs?

When there are two giraffes!

Elephant 1: Did you hear about the race between the two giraffes?
Elephant 2: I heard it was neck and neck!

How does a lion greet the other animals in the savannah?

"Pleased to eat you!"

What time is it when an elephant sits on your fence?

Time to fix the fence.

What do you call a rhino at the North Pole?

Lost.

Knock, knock.
Who's there?
Rhino.
Rhino who?
Rhino every knock-knock joke there is.

What do elephants do for laughs?
They tell people jokes.

If the alphabet goes from *A* to *Z*, what goes from *Z* to *A*?

A zebra.

Where do Italian elephants live?

Tusk-any.

What is black and white and black and white and black and white?

A zebra in a revolving door.

Justin: Pretend you are in Africa and a cheetah is chasing you. What do you do?

Jenna: Stop pretending!

How do elephants talk to each other?

They call on the elephone.

A lion was playing checkers with a cheetah. The cheetah skipped across the board and got all the checkers in one move. "You're a cheetah!" said the lion. "You're lion!" said the cheetah.

What did the elephant say when he saw something gross?

"That is 'grotusk'!"

Which state do lions like best?

Maine (mane).

What kind of illness can a zebra get?

Stripe throat.

What do you call an animal that never takes a bath?

A smellyphant.

What do you call a hippo in a phone booth?

Stuck.

Why did the elephant sit on the marshmallow?

So he wouldn't fall into the hot chocolate.

What do you need to know if you want to be a lion tamer?

More than the lion.

Knock, knock.
Who's there?
Lionel.
Lionel who?
Lionel bite you if you put your head in its mouth.

Dino Laughs

What do you get if you give a dinosaur a pogo stick?

Big holes in your driveway.

What do you get if you cross a dinosaur and a football player?

A quarterback no one can tackle.

What do you call a dinosaur with an extensive vocabulary?

A thesaurus.

Aiden: What do you call a nearsighted dinosaur?
Zoey: I don't know. What?
Aiden: Doyathinkhesaurus.
Zoey: Well then, what do you call his dog?
Aiden: Doyouthinkhesaurus Rex.

What is a dinosaur's favorite snack?

Macaroni and trees.

What type of tool does a prehistoric reptile carpenter use?

A dino-saw.

What do you call a sleeping prehistoric reptile?

A dinosnore.

What kind of dinosaur has no wings, but flies all over?

One that needs a bath.

What dinosaur could jump higher than a house?

All of them—houses can't jump.

What do you get if you cross a dinosaur with a kangaroo?

A tricera-hops.

Knock, Knock.
Who's There?
Dinosaur.
Dinosaur who?
Dinosaurs don't go who. They go ROAR!

What did dinosaurs use to make their hot dogs?

Jurassic pork.

Knock, knock.
Who's there?
T. rex.
T. rex who?
There's a *T. rex* at your door and you want to know its name?!

Why did the Bambiraptor say "knock, knock"?

Because it was in the wrong joke.

What do you call a dinosaur when it wears a cowboy hat and boots?

Tyrannosaurus tex.

What do you say to a ten-ton dinosaur wearing earphones?

Whatever you like—he can't hear you.

When can three brontosauruses hide under a small umbrella and not get wet?

When it's not raining!

What do you ask a thirsty tyrannosaur?

"Tea, Rex?"

Mom: Trent, if you don't stop banging that drum, I'll go out of my mind.
Trent: Too late, Mom. I stopped an hour ago.

Funny Family

Dad: What was that loud noise?

Jack: My jacket fell on the floor.

Dad: Why would your jacket make such a loud noise?

Jack: Because I was wearing it.

What did the boy use to keep track of his mother?

A ther-mom-eter.

Mom: Would you like an apple?

Clara: I don't feel like an apple today.

Mom: That's good. You don't look like an apple either.

Boy: Doctor! Doctor! My sister is invisible!

Doctor: What sister?

Mom: Dan, you've lost your two front teeth.

Dan: Oh, no, I haven't, Mom. I have them in my pocket.

Why does the mom carry the baby?

Because the baby can't carry the mom.

What did the snake say to his little sister?

"Stop being such a rattle-tail!"

Mom: What was that big crash, honey?

Liam: You know that vase you were worried I'd break?

Mom: Yes, I remember.

Liam: Well, your worries are over.

If you eat two-thirds of a pie, what do you have?

An angry mom.

How did the grandmother knit a suit of armor?

She used steel wool.

Mom: Did you thank Mrs. Smith for the lovely party she gave?

Audrey: No, Mom. The girls leaving before me thanked her, and Mrs. Smith said, "Don't mention it." So I didn't.

Julia: Mom! There's a monster under my bed!

Mom: Tell him to get back in the closet where he belongs.

Dad: Did you eat all the cookies in the cookie jar?

Hope: No, I didn't touch one.

Dad: Then why is there only one left?

Hope: That's the one I didn't touch.

If grown-ups have knees, what do kids have?

Kid-knees.

Kylee: Happy birthday, Grandma!

Grandma: Why did you give me a bunch of scrap paper?

Kylee: Because I love you to pieces!

What did the chimpanzee say when he found out his sister had a baby?

"Well, I'll be a monkey's uncle!"

Henry: Dad, I can't . . .

Dad: Henry, never say you can't do something.

Henry: OK. Then will you help me put the toothpaste back in the tube?

Mom: Tommy, please pick up your room.

Tommy: I don't think I'm strong enough.

Mom: What are you doing?

Jesse: I'm washing my hands.

Mom: Without soap and water?

Jesse: Haven't you heard of dry cleaning?

Eli: Why does your grandmother have roller skates on her rocking chair?

Emily: She likes to rock and roll.

Who did Antarctica marry?

Uncle Arctica.

What does it mean when you come into the house and you don't have to do any chores?

You're in the wrong house.

What did the boy with the world's greatest mom do?

He built her a mom-ument.

What did the father buffalo say to his kid when he dropped him off at school?

"Bison."

Aunt Cora: Jeremy, you know you should have given the bigger piece of cake to your little sister. Haven't you noticed that a mother hen gives the fattest worm to the littlest chick?

Jeremy: Sure. And I would have, too, if it had been a worm!

Amusing Music

What do musicians do when they lose their beat?

They have a tempo-tantrum.

What does a musician use to brush his teeth?

A tuba toothpaste.

What is a woodwind player's favorite dessert?

Flutecake.

Why did the robot win the dance contest?

He was a dancing machine.

What kind of toy likes to rap?

A yo-yo.

Why couldn't the piano get back into his house?

Because he lost his keys.

What did the guitar say to the musician?

Stop picking on me!

What is an elf's favorite music?

Gift rap.

Why did Mozart get rid of his chickens?

They kept saying, "Bach, Bach, Bach."

What do you call a group of people playing bendable musical instruments?

A rubber band.

What dessert would you feed to a string quartet?

Cell-O.

Violinist: When can I use the practice room?
Pianist: I'll be out in a minuet.

What kind of music did the Pilgrims like?

Plymouth Rock.

Knock, knock.

Who's there?

Sonata.

Sonata who?

Don't worry, sonata a big deal.

Composer: It took me ten years to write this lullaby.

Publisher: Why did it take so long?

Composer: It kept putting me to sleep.

Piano Tuner: I'm here to tune your piano.

Marcy: I didn't call for a piano tuner.

Piano Tuner: I know. Your neighbors did.

What is a cow's favorite subject in school?

Moo-sic.

What kind of music do hammocks like?

Rock.

What kind of music do they play on a space shuttle?

Rocket roll.

What is a balloon's least favorite music?

Pop.

Jill: Was that you singing when I came in?

Jan: Yes. I was killing time before my lesson.

Jill: Well, you were definitely using the right weapon.

Pat: I once sang "The Star-Spangled Banner" for three hours nonstop.

Shannon: That's nothing. I can sing "Stars and Stripes Forever."

Why did people dance when the vegetable band played?

The music had a good beet.

Why did the music teacher need a ladder?

To reach the high notes.

What did the conductor say to the orchestra?

"We've got a score to settle."

Why did the musician break his new CD?

He wanted his song to be a smash hit.

Knock, knock.
Who's there?
Little old lady.
Little old lady who?
I didn't know you could yodel!

What's green and sings?

Elvis Parsley.

Which instrument never tells the truth?

A lyre.

Which parts of the body are the most musical?

The organs.

How are a train and an orchestra alike?

They both have conductors.

What is a musical note's favorite sport?

Beat boxing.

What is the trombone's favorite thing on the playground?

The slide.

What do playing the piano and running too fast have in common?

If you don't C sharp, you will B flat.

Where did the whale play his violin?

In the orca-stra.

How does the heart play music?

It follows the beat.

What kind of meat do singers like to eat?

So-la-mi.

If lightning strikes an orchestra, who is most likely to get hit?

The conductor.

Jessica: Why are you plucking your guitar strings with a pencil?

Joshua: I'm trying to write a song.

Customer: I'd like to buy that piano. Does it come with a guarantee?
Clerk: I can guarantee it's a piano.

What is a rock star's favorite food?

Jam.

Baylor: Why do you keep your MP3 player in the refrigerator?

Taylor: Because I like cool music!

Why were the musical notes upset?

Because they were right next to the trouble (treble) clef.

Space for Laughs

What do aliens eat for breakfast?

Flying sausages.

What does outer space have in common with basketball?

They both have shooting stars.

How do you know when the moon is broke?

When it's down to its last quarter.

How do you get a baby astronaut to sleep?

You rocket.

How do you tie your shoes in outer space?

With an astroknot.

How does the man on the moon hold up his pants?

With an asteroid belt.

First Astronaut: Get ready for launch.
Second Astronaut: But I haven't had breakfast yet.

What was the first animal in space?

The cow that jumped over the moon.

Where do aliens keep their coffee cups?

On flying saucers.

How does an alien count to twenty-three?

On its fingers.

How do you have a good outer-space party?

Planet.

What are the solar system's three favorite days of the week?

Saturnday, Sunday, and Moonday.

What holds the sun up in the sky?

Sunbeams.

Where do astronauts go to study?

The mooniversity.

What is the Earth after it rotates all day?

Dizzy.

Why does the moon go to the bank?

To change quarters.

What does one star say to another when they pass by?

"Glad to meteor."

First astronaut: If you look down, I think you can see China.
Second astronaut: You've got to be kidding. The next thing I know, you'll tell me I can see knives and forks, too!

What do you say to a two-headed space alien?

"Hello, hello!"

Why didn't the sun go to college?

Because it already had thousands of degrees.

Sam: Did you hear the joke about the rocket?
Ben: No, what is it?
Sam: It's out of this world!

Don: Can you telephone from a space shuttle?
Dan: Of course I can tell a phone from a space shuttle!

What is an astronaut's favorite key on the keyboard?

The space bar.

What did the dentist call the astronaut's cavity?

A black hole.

What do moon men call French fries?

Crater taters.

First Astronaut: What's that thing in the frying pan?
Second Astronaut: It's an unidentified frying object.

Why do hamburgers taste better in outer space?

Because they're meteor.

What do planets do for fun?

Sing Neptunes.

What blooms in outer space?

Sunflowers.

What did the meteor mom say to her muddy son?

Take a meteor shower.

Who is Saturn?

The lord of the rings.

How is Saturn like a jewelry box?

It has rings.

What happens when an astronaut lets go of his sundae?

He gets an ice-cream float.

What did the astronomer do when his theory was proved correct?

He thanked his lucky stars.

Where do astronauts store their food?

In launch boxes.

How is food served in space?

In satellite dishes.

Why should you never insult a Martian?

It might get its feelers hurt.

What sound does a space turkey make?

"Hubble, hubble, hubble."

Why didn't the rocket have a job?

Because it was fired.

What are the clumsiest things in the galaxy?

Falling stars.

Why did the moon stop eating?

It was full.

Why did the astronaut go to the foot doctor?

She had missile toe.

What do Martians who use the metric system say when they land on Earth?

Take me to your liter.

How does the man in the moon get his hair cut?

Eclipse it.

How did Mary's little lamb get to Mars?

By rocket sheep.

What did the comet say to the sun?

"See you next time around!"

What do astronauts use to brush their teeth?

Toothspace.

What does Saturn like to read?

Comet books.

Knock, knock.

Who's there?

Comet.

Comet who?

Comet a crime, go to jail.

What did one rocketship say to the other?

"Give me some space!"

Silly School

Teacher: Where's your homework, Zach?
Zach: I don't have it. My dog ate it.
Teacher: How could your dog eat your homework?
Zach: I fed it to him.

How do you get straight A's?

By using a ruler.

What do you call a pirate who skips school?

Captain Hooky.

What kind of candy is always late for class?

Choco-late.

What is an art teacher's favorite fruit?

Crayonberries.

Why did the clock in the cafeteria always run slow?

Every lunch it went back four seconds.

What is a teacher's favorite country?

Expla-nation.

Why did the teacher go to the beach?

To test the water.

What do elves do after school?

Gnomework.

Ann: Hooray! The teacher said we will have a test, rain or shine.

Dan: Then why are you so happy?

Ann: It's snowing!

Dad: What did you learn in school today?
Son: Not enough. I have to go back tomorrow!

What would you get if you crossed a vampire and a teacher?

Lots of blood tests.

What do you call a teacher who never says your name right?

Miss Pronounce.

What's the best place to grow flowers in school?

In kinder-garden.

Why did the chicken stay home from school?

It had the people pox.

244

Why did the dollar do so well in school?

He was paying attention.

What did the boy snail say to the girl snail at the school dance?

"I'm really good at slow dancing."

Why did the boy bring a ladder to school?

He wanted to go to high school.

Why was the cafeteria's kitchen having math problems?

Its counter was gone.

What do you do if a teacher rolls her eyes at you?

Pick them up and roll them back to her.

What did the ghost teacher say to the class?

Look at the board and I will go through it again.

Teacher: Why didn't you finish your homework?
Monster: I was full.

Knock, knock.
Who's there?
Ketchup.
Ketchup who?
Ketchup or else you'll miss the school bus!

Knock, knock.

Who's there?

Needle.

Needle who?

Needle little help with your homework?

What did the cat teacher say to the cat student?

You have a purrrrfect score!

Why did the teacher wear sunglasses in school?

Because his class was so bright.

What is an English teacher's favorite breakfast?

A synonym roll.

What do you call a duck that gets all A's in school?

A wise quacker.

What is a pirate's favorite subject?

Arrrrt.

What is a robot's favorite part of school?

Assembly.

Why was the math teacher crying on the last day of school?

Because he didn't want to be divided from his students.

Why didn't the nose want to go to school?

Because he didn't want to get picked on.

Why did the teacher fall in love with the janitor?

Because he swept her off her feet.

Why did the teacher draw on the window?

Because he wanted his lesson to be clear.

Why did the boy eat his homework?

Because the teacher said it was a piece of cake.

Teacher: How many letters are in the alphabet?
Student: 11.
Teacher: No, there are 26. How did you get 11?
Student: T-H-E A-L-P-H-A-B-E-T.

Teacher: Liza, what is your favorite state?
Liza: Mississippi.
Teacher: Spell it, please.
Liza: Oh, favorite state? I meant to say Ohio.

What's the hardest thing about falling out of bed on the first day of school?

The floor.

What's bacteria?

The rear entrance to a cafeteria.

Which school supply is king of the classroom?

The ruler.

Why did the light bulb go to school?

He wanted to get brighter.

What has forty feet and sings?

The school choir.

Why did the kid study in the airplane?

He wanted a higher education.

What's the difference between a teacher and a train?

The teacher says, "Spit out your gum," and the train says, "Choo-choo."

Why did the student bring scissors to school?

He wanted to cut class.

Why did the girl bring her dad's credit card to school?

She wanted extra credit.

Why did the student do multiplication problems on the floor?

The teacher told her not to use tables.

What do vampires wear on the first day of school?

Their bat-to-school clothes.

How is a language arts teacher like a judge?

They both give out sentences.

What do math teachers do in the lunchroom?

They divide their lunches with one another.

What happened when the teacher tied all the kids' shoelaces together?

They had a class trip.

Evan: I got 100 in school today.

Dad: That's great! In what subject?

Evan: I got 50 in spelling and 50 in math.

Why do soccer players do so well in school?

They use their heads.

Why did the dad have to go to school?

To take his pop quiz.

What do you say when comforting a grammar teacher?

"There, their, they're."

What did the cheese say when he got his school picture taken?

"People!"

Mark: Do you like homework?

Marietta: I like nothing better.

What kind of school do air and water go to?

Element-ary school.

Mom: What did you learn in school today?
Lila: My teacher taught us writing.
Mom: What did you write?
Lila: I don't know. She hasn't taught us reading yet.

What do school librarians use as bait when they go fishing?

Bookworms.

What did the student say after the teacher said, "Order in the classroom"?

"I'll have a burger and fries, please."

Why is history the fruitiest subject in school?

Because it's full of dates.

Who invented algebra?

An X-pert.

What topping do teachers put on their pizza?

Graded cheese.

Why did the new boy steal a chair from the classroom?

Because the teacher told him to take a seat.

What did the sweet potato say to the teacher?

"Here I yam!"

Why are school cafeteria workers so mean?

Because they batter fish, beat eggs, and whip cream.

When is a blue schoolbook not a blue schoolbook?

When it is read.

Why is arithmetic hard work?

You have to carry all those numerals

Patrick: Dad, Mrs. Jones gave me an *F* for this drawing.

Dad: She did? That's a great drawing! Why would she give you an *F*?

Patrick: Because I drew it in French class.

Why was the child's report card all wet?

Because it was under C-level.

When does a teacher carry birdseed?

When she has a parrot-teacher conference.

Teacher: Now class, I will ask you a question, and I want you all to answer at once. What is 7 plus 8?

Class: At once!

Teacher: Where is your homework?

Boy: A ghost ate it.

Teacher: I can see right through that excuse!

What did the mom chameleon say to her nervous kid on the first day of school?

"Don't worry, you'll blend right in!"

What did the bubble gum say when it failed its test?

"I blew it."

Hector: The music teacher said I should sing tenor.

Mom: Tenor?

Hector: Ten or eleven miles away.

How can you tell a school bus from a grape?

Jump on one for a while. If you don't get any juice, it's a school bus.

Jennifer: Why were you late for school today?

Jeremy: I was dreaming about a football game, and it went into overtime.

Dad: Dave, were you late for school again?

Dave: Yes, but didn't Miss Jones say that it's never too late to learn?

Kara: My mom says that I get to choose my school clothes this year.

Sara: Oh, really? My dog's the one that chews mine!

Micah: School is so confusing!

Dad: Why?

Micah: Ms. Peterson said, "One plus nine equals ten, six plus four equals ten, and seven plus three equals ten."

Dad: So?

Micah: She won't make up her mind!

Tara: Why weren't you in school today?

Daryl: I had a toothache, so I went to the dentist.

Tara: Does your tooth still ache?

Daryl: I don't know. The dentist kept it.

Why was the dog so good in school?

Because he was the teacher's pet.

Mom: Why didn't you take the school bus home?

Andy: I tried, but it wouldn't fit in my backpack.

School Nurse: Have your eyes ever been checked?

Student: No, they've always been blue.

Why did the clock go to the principal's office?

For tocking too much.

Teacher: Ashley, name two pronouns.

Ashley: Who, me?

Teacher: That's correct.

Teacher: Give me a sentence starting with I.

Student: OK. I is . . .

Teacher: No, no. You do not say "I is. " You say "I am. "

Student: OK. I am the ninth letter of the alphabet.

Why was the math book sad?

Because it had too many problems.

Why did the phone move up a grade in school?

Because it was a smartphone.

What is the worst thing that can happen to a geography teacher?

Getting lost.

What did Natasha do when she saw the class rabbit eating the dictionary?

She took the words right out of his mouth.

Teacher: Stephanie, where is Moscow?
Stephanie: In the barn next to Pa's cow.

Why did the girl wear glasses during math class?

Because it improves di-vision.

What kind of meals do math teachers eat?

Square meals.

What will the school for race cars do after the summer?

Re-zoom.

What do baby bunnies learn in school?

The alfalfa-bet.

What vegetables do school librarians like?

Quiet peas.

What is a school librarian's favorite food to barbecue?

Shush-kabob.

What did the lobster give to its teacher?

A crab apple.

Ticklish Travel

What is a mushroom's favorite vacation spot?

Port-a-Bella.

Where is the best place to eat while traveling?

Where there's a fork in the road.

Knock, knock.
Who's there?
Earl.
Earl who?
Earl be glad when vacation starts.

Where do termites go on vacation?

Hollywood.

Where do cars go on vacation?

Key West.

A family of pickles is about to drive across the country for a vacation.

Baby Pickle: What if we have car trouble?

Mom Pickle: It'll be OK. We'll just dill with it!

Tory: There are sixty fish in a fish tank. Twenty go on vacation. How many are left?

Leah: Well, sixty minus twenty is—

Tory: Stop counting. Fish don't go on vacation!

Where did the pencil go for vacation?

Pennsylvania.

Tyler: I just flew in from Philadelphia.
Dylan: Wow! Your arms must be tired.

How do rabbits travel?

By hareplane.

Why did the sheep jump over the moon?

Because the cow was on vacation.

Where does bacon go on vacation?

The Pigcific Ocean.

Why did the elephant get upset on vacation?

He forgot to pack his trunk.

Why did the egg go to the jungle on vacation?

He wanted to be an egg-splorer.

How do snowmen travel around?

By icicle.

Which mountain is the laziest?

Mount Ever-rest.

Where are the Great Plains?

At the great airports.

What's purple, long, and 50,000 years old?

The Grape Wall of China.

Where do birds stay when they're on vacation?

At a cheep hotel.

Where do shoelaces go on vacation?

Tie-land (Thailand).

Knock, knock.
Who's there?
Tree.
Tree who?
Tree more days till vacation.

Kid: Where did the sneakers go on vacation?
Parent: I don't know. Where?
Kid: Lace Vegas!

What state is round at each end and high in the middle?
Ohio.

How did the locomotive learn to run on tracks?
It trained for it.

Two wrongs do not make a right. But what do two rights make?
The first airplane.

What did the car wheels say after a long drive?
"We're tired out!"

Where do pirates go on vacation?

AAARRRgentina.

Knock, knock.
Who's there?
Florida.
Florida who?
The Florida bathroom is wet

What is the coldest country in South America?

Chile.

Where do ghosts go for a vacation?

The Boohamas.

Where does bacteria go on vacation?

Germany.

How do you find out the weather when you're on vacation?

Look out the window.

Brittany: Which famous structure keeps falling?
Teacher: The Leaning Tower of Pisa?
Brittany: No, the I-fell (Eiffel) Tower.

Teacher: Johnny, what are the four seasons?
Johnny: Baseball, football, hockey, and vacation!

How can you drive two thousand miles with a flat tire?

Your spare tire is flat—the four you're riding on are fine.

Household Humor

Why did the boy take wood, screws, a hammer, nails, a screwdriver, a pillow, and a blanket up to his room?

He wanted to make his bed.

What kind of clothing does a house wear?

An address.

Why did the onion go to the other onion's house?

Because they were having a family re-onion.

What did one wall say to the other wall?

"Meet you at the corner."

What do you call a lawyer's house?

A legal pad.

What's the best side of the house to put the porch on?

The outside.

What is a door's favorite kind of joke?

A knock-knock.

What do you call singing in the shower?

A soap opera.

What did the bald man say when he got a comb for his birthday?

"Thanks, I'll never part with it."

What did one broom say to the other broom at bedtime?

"Sweep tight."

What did one camera say to the other when it saw something interesting?

"That's flashinating."

What did the picture say to the wall?

"I've got you covered."

What did the happy light bulb say to the sad light bulb?

"Why don't you lighten up?"

What did the tie say to the hat?

"You go on ahead and I'll hang around."

What do chairs use to hold up their pants?

Seat belts.

Knock, knock.
Who's there?
Isabel.
Isabel who?
Isabel on your house working?

What does an expensive TV have in common with a dictionary on top of a mountain?

They're both high definition.

Where do books sleep?

Under their covers.

Mom: Josh, did you take a shower this morning?

Josh: Why, is there one missing?

Why did the boy put cheese beside the computer?

To feed the mouse.

Why did the dust bunny use the computer?

To go on the linternet.

When is a door not a door?

When it's a jar.

What kind of coat is always wet when you put it on?

A coat of paint.

What do snakes put on their kitchen floors?

Reptiles.

Knock, knock.
Who's there?
Clothesline.
Clothesline who?
**Clothesline all over the floor end
up wrinkled.**

What did one candle say to the other candle?

"Are you going out tonight?"

What did the sandal say to the sneaker?

"Don't stick your tongue out at me!"

What did the carpet say to the ceiling?

"I look up to you."

Knock, knock.
Who's there?
House.
House who?
Hi, house you doing?

What gets wetter the more it dries?

A towel.

What has a foot on each side and one in the middle?

A yardstick.

Katie: Why did the chicken cross the road?
Michael: I don't know. Why?
Katie: To get to your house. Knock, knock.
Michael: Who's there?
Katie: The chicken, silly!

Where can everyone find money?

In the dictionary.

What is bought by the yard and worn by the foot?

A carpet.

What has teeth but can't eat?

A comb.

What is full of holes but can still hold water?

A sponge.

What's another name for a grandfather clock?

An old-timer.

Why did the computer cross the road?

It wanted to get with the program.

What did the digital clock say to the grandfather clock?

"Look, Grandpa—no hands!"

What does one clock say to another clock on its birthday?

"You're getting older by the minute."

Why did the cat lie on the computer?

To keep an eye on the mouse.

How does a polar bear build its house?

Igloos it together.

Wacky Weather and Silly Seasons

What's worse than raining cats and dogs?

Hailing taxis.

What is a tornado's favorite game?

Twister.

What does a rain cloud wear under its clothes?

Thunderwear.

What did summer say to spring?

"Help! I'm going to fall."

What do clouds and cowboys have in common?

They both hold the reins.

What's a math teacher's favorite season?

Summer.

The little tree got worried in October because all his leaves fell off. But when spring came, he was re-leaved.

What did one hurricane say to the other?

"I have my eye on you."

Knock, knock.
Who's there?
Summertime.
Summertime who?
Summertime you can be really funny.

What time of year is it best to use a trampoline?

In the springtime.

What do you call sleeping twisters?

Tornadoze.

Why does lightning shock people?

Because it doesn't know how to conduct itself.

Knock, knock.
Who's there?
Sleet.
Sleet who?
Sleet—I'm starving.

How does a hippopotamus get down from a tree?

It sits on a leaf and waits for the fall.

Abby: Where are you going with that watering can?

Wyatt: Out to water my flowers.

Abby: But it's raining.

Wyatt: OK, I'll wear my raincoat.

Knock, knock.
Who's there?
Accordion.
Accordion who?
Accordion the weather report, it's
going to rain tomorrow.

What do you call a goose that stays up north for the winter?

A brrrrd.

What do you get when you tie a ribbon on a horse's bridle?

A reinbow.

What did the raindrop say when it fell?

"Oops, I dripped!"

Knock, knock.
Who's there?
Scold.
Scold who?
Scold outside.

Knock, knock.
Who's there?
Wet.
Wet who?
Wet me in—it's waining

What is the opposite of a hurricane?

A him-icane.

What do you call it when it rains chickens and ducks?

Fowl weather.

What do snowmen wear on their heads?

Ice caps.

What did one snowman say to the other?

"Is it me, or do you smell carrots?"

What happened to the wind?

It blew away.

What did one tornado say to the other?

"Let's twist again like we did last summer."

Knock, knock.
Who's there?
Emma.
Emma who?
Emma bit cold out here.
Please let me in.

What's the difference between a horse and the weather?

One is reined up and the other rains down.

What do clouds wear in their hair?

Rainbows.

What is a snowman's favorite lunch?

An iceberger.

Where do snowpeople dance?

At a snowball.

Why should you never tell a joke while ice fishing?

Because the ice will crack up.

What is the coldest month of the year?

Decem-brrrr.

Why was there thunder and lightning in the science lab?

The scientists were brainstorming.

Knock, knock.
Who's there?
Guitar.
Guitar who?
Let's guitar coats—it's cold outside.

What happened when the snowwoman got angry at the snowman?

She gave him the cold shoulder.

Why did Avery go outside with her purse open?

She was expecting some change in the weather.

What's the difference between weather and climate?

You can't weather a tree, but you can climate.

Why do birds fly south in the winter?

It's too far to walk.

What do polar bears do on the computer?

They surf the Winternet.

Hysterical History

What do you get when you cross a U.S. president with a shark?

Jaws Washington.

Where did people dance in medieval times?

In knight clubs.

How many ears did Davy Crockett have?

Three—a left ear, a right ear, and a wild frontier.

Why does the Statue of Liberty stand in New York harbor?

Because it can't sit down.

Mom: Why aren't you doing well in history?

Marley: Because the teacher keeps asking about things that happened before I was born.

How did the Vikings send secret messages?

By Norse code.

Teacher: What did they do at the Boston Tea Party?

Max: I don't know—I wasn't invited.

What does the president hang in the White House on the Fourth of July?

The Decoration of Independence.

Where were English kings usually crowned?

On the head.

Who succeeded the first president of the United States?

The second one.

What did Benjamin Franklin say when he flew a kite in a lightning storm?

Nothing—he was too shocked.

What did George Washington say to his men before they crossed the Delaware?

"Get in the boat, men."

How did Noah see at night on the ark?

Floodlights.

Why were the early days of history called the Dark Ages?

Because there were so many knights.

How do you find King Arthur in the dark?

With a knight light.

How did Columbus's men sleep on their ships?

With their eyes shut.

Which president was the most environmentally aware?

Treeodore Roosevelt.

What did Mason say to Dixon?

"We've got to draw the line here."

Knock, knock.
Who's there?
Tarzan.
Tarzan who?
Tarzan stripes forever.

Why did the pioneers cross the country in covered wagons?

Because they didn't want to wait forty years for a train.

What famous inventor enjoyed practical jokes?

Benjamin Pranklin.

Why is England the wettest country?

Because the queen has reigned there for years.

What did Paul Revere say when his ride was over?

"Whoa!"

Why did George Washington wear red, white, and blue suspenders?

To hold up his pants.

What explorer was the best at hide-and-seek?

Marco Polo.

Why did Arthur have a round table?

So no one could corner him!

What do Alexander the Great and Winnie the Pooh have in common?

They have the same middle name.

What do presidents eat to freshen their breath?

Govern-mints.

What was purple and conquered the world?

Alexander the Grape.

Dad: How is your report card, Maria?

Maria: Well, Dad, I did the same thing as George Washington.

Dad: And what is that?

Maria: I went down in history.

Teacher: For homework tonight, I want you to write an essay on Abraham Lincoln.

Joey: I'd rather write on paper.

Who un-invented the airplane?

The Wrong brothers.

Candice: Why was the pharaoh boastful?

Larry: I don't know. Why?

Candice: Because he sphinx he's the best.

Maggie: I wish I had been born 1000 years ago.

Cassie: Why is that?

Maggie: Just think of all the history that I wouldn't have to learn!

If April showers bring May flowers, what do May flowers bring?

Pilgrims.

Ted: What's the difference between a duck and George Washington?

Bob: I don't know. What?

Ted: A duck has a bill on its face, and George Washington has his face on a bill.

What was the most popular dance in 1776?

Indepen-dance.

What did Paul Revere say when he went to the orthodontist?

"The braces are coming! The braces are coming!"

Natasha: Did you know that Abraham Lincoln had to walk miles to school every day?
Nathan: Well, he should have gotten up earlier and caught the school bus like everyone else!

Who invented fractions?

Henry the 1/4th.

What explorer was the best at hide-and-seek?

Marco Polo.

How were the first Americans like ants?

They lived in colonies.

Teacher: What was Camelot?
Adam: A place where people parked their camels.

Teacher: What important event happened in 1809?

Matt: Abraham Lincoln was born.

Teacher: Correct. Now what important event happened in 1812?

Matt: Abraham Lincoln had his third birthday.

Which American president wore the biggest hat?

The one with the biggest head.

Lara: Did you hear the one about the Liberty Bell?

Lance: Yeah, it cracked me up, too!

Why was it easy to celebrate Mother's Day in Ancient Egypt?

Because there were so many mummies.

Knock, knock.
Who's there?
General Lee.
General Lee who?
General Lee, I do not tell knock-knock jokes.

One day, a man asked the President of the United States if he could have the country for free. The president said no.
"Why not?" the man asked. "I thought it was a free country!"

Where was the Declaration of Independence signed?

At the bottom.

What do you call an American drawing?

A Yankee doodle.

Why did the Dalmatian go to the eye doctor?

He was seeing spots.

Why did the pickle go to the doctor?

He felt dill.

A doctor looks into a patient's ear.
Doctor: I think I see a whole herd of elephants in there!
Patient: Herd of elephants?
Doctor: Of course I've heard of elephants. Haven't you?

Why did the cookie go to the doctor?

He felt crumby.

What should you do if your poodle won't stop sneezing?

Call a dogtor.

Patient: I have butterflies in my stomach.
Doctor: Did you take an aspirin?
Patient: Yes, and now they're playing Ping-Pong.

Patient: Doctor, help! I'm shrinking!
Doctor: Calm down. You're just going to have to be a little patient.

What should you do if you break your arm in two places?

Stay away from those places.

One day while crossing the road, a snail was hit by a turtle. At the hospital, the doctor asked, "How did it happen?" "I can't remember," said the snail. "It all happened so fast."

Ben: Doctor, it hurts when I touch here and here and here. What's wrong with me?

Doctor: Your finger is broken.

Doctor: Well, Susan, your cough seems to be better today than it was yesterday.

Susan: It should be! I've been practicing all night.

Where did the soda go when it lost its bubbles?

To the fizzician.

Fred: Have you heard about the guy whose left side fell off?

Ted: No, how is he doing?

Fred: He's all right now!

What is hairy and coughs?

A coconut with a cold

Why did Mr. and Mrs. Tonsil dress up?

Because the doctor was taking them out.

Grace: Have you heard the one about the germ?

Mya: No.

Grace: Never mind . . . I don't want it to spread.

Patient: Doctor, I have a carrot growing out of my ear!

Doctor: How could this have happened?

Patient: I don't know. I planted cabbages!

Man: Doctor! Doctor! I need some glasses!

Waiter: You sure do. This is a restaurant.

Nurse: Doctor, there's a ghost in the waiting room.

Doctor: Tell him I can't see him.

What kind of wild animal might you find in a dentist's office?

A molar bear.

What's another name for a dentist's office?

A filling station.

What is the best time to go to the dentist?

Tooth-hurty.

What do you do when your tooth falls out?

Use the toothpaste.

What is a dentist's favorite game?

Tooth or dare.

Optometrist: You need glasses.
Patient: How can you tell?
Optometrist: I noticed when you walked through the window.

Patient: I feel like a deck of cards.
Doctor: Wait here. I'll deal with you later.

Patient: Nurse, Nurse! I was playing my harmonica, and I swallowed it.

Nurse: You're lucky you weren't playing a piano!

Boy: Do you make house calls?

Doctor: Yes, but your house has to be really sick.

Patient: Doctor, why are some jokes so painfully funny?

Doctor: It must be the punch line.

Girl: Doctor, my Lego blocks are broken. What do you recommend?

Doctor: Plastic surgery.

What does an onion a day do?

It keeps everyone away.

Camper: Doctor, that ointment you gave me makes my arm smart.

Doctor: In that case, rub some on your head.

How does a pig get to the hospital?

In a hambulance.

What illness can you catch from a martial-arts expert?

Kung flu.

What did the doctor give the pig for its rash?

Oinkment.

Who does a mallard visit when he feels sick?

A ducktor.

What is the best kind of book to read when you have a cold?

Sinus fiction.

Doctor: Did you ask the patient his name so we can notify his family?

Nurse: He says his family already knows his name.

Doctor: I'm getting angry!

Nurse: Well, don't lose your patients.

What do you give a sick relative?

Auntiebiotics.

Patient: It hurts every time I raise my arm. What should I do?

Doctor: Don't raise your arm.

Nurse: May I take your pulse?

Patient: Why? Haven't you got one of your own?

What is the difference between a hill and a pill?

A hill is hard to get up, and a pill is hard to get down.

Why did the book go to the doctor?

Because it hurt its spine.

Doctor: Why do you look so tired?

Patient: I stayed up all night studying for my blood test.

Patient: Are tomatoes healthy?

Doctor: I've never heard one complain.

Patient: Doctor, what should I do when my ear rings?

Doctor: Answer it!

What did the doctor say to the woman who swallowed a spoon?

"Sit still and don't stir."

What did one elevator say to the other?

"I think I'm coming down with something."

What did the doctor say to the frog?

"You need a hoperation."

Mother: Why do you want to be a doctor, Sally?

Sally: I wanted to be a teacher, but I don't have enough patience. I decided that I would be a doctor because then I can have all the patients I want.

Doctor: Here is a joke book.
Patient: That won't cure my cold!
Doctor: Laughter is the best medicine.

Goofy Grab Bag

Larry: What does IDK mean?
Mitch: I don't know.
Larry: You're the fifth person I've asked. Nobody knows what it means!

Knock, knock.
Who's there?
Cash.
Cash who?
No thanks, I prefer peanuts.

What do you call a yo-yo without a string?

A no-yo.

What do you call a boomerang that doesn't come back to you?

A bummerang.

What did the ambitious elevator say to his mom?

"Things are looking up."

Why didn't the square talk to the circle?

Because there wasn't a point.

What makes the tooth fairy so smart?

Wisdom teeth.

How do rodents freshen their breath?

With mousewash.

One eye said to the other eye, "Just between the two of us, there's something that smells."

What is a song about a car called?

A car tune.

What kind of bus has two floors and says, "Quack"?

A double ducker.

What does a car wear on its head?

A gas cap.

What kind of locomotive needs a tissue?

An ah-choo-choo train.

How do stairs travel?

By flight.

What do you get when you cross a piece of paper with a pair of scissors?

A paper cut.

What did the O say to the 8?

"Hey, nice belt!"

What is a pronoun?

A noun that gets paid.

What do you call more than one L?

A parallel.

What geometric figure is like a lost parrot?

A polygon.

Why couldn't orange stay in rhythm with the other colors?

Because red and yellow were mixing him up.

What do you get when you throw books into the ocean?

A title wave.

Why can't your nose be 12 inches long?

Because then it would be a foot.

Knock, knock.
Who's there?
Ear.
Ear who?
Ear you are. I've been looking everywhere!

What's green and smells like blue paint?

Green paint.

Why didn't the scientist put a bell on his door?

He wanted to win the no-bell prize.

Why was the karate teacher arrested at the butcher shop?

He was caught choplifting.

Where do geologists like to relax?

In rocking chairs.

Where do joggers take baths?

In running water.

Why is an ice cube so smart?

It has 32 degrees.

How does a tree draw a person?

It makes a stick figure.

What kind of books do mountain climbers like to read?

Cliffhangers.

Why is lava red hot?

Because if it were cold and white, it would be snow.

What happened to the frog that parked illegally?

He got toad.

Why did the traffic light turn red?

You would, too, if you had to change in the middle of the street.

What comes after *L*?

Bow.

What kind of gum do scientists chew?

Ex-spearmint gum.

Why did the boy stare at his carton of orange juice?

Because it said, "Concentrate."

Dana: What would you do if you were trapped on an iceberg?
Matt: Just chill.

What do you call a boy with a dictionary in his back pocket?

Smartypants.

Why did the germ cross the microscope?

To get to the other slide.

Why did the chicken cross the book?

To get to the author side.

What is heavy forward but not backward?

Ton.

Knock, knock.
Who's there?
Mozart.
Mozart who?
Mozart is found in museums.

What kind of plant is good at gymnastics?

Tumbleweed.

What did the cowboy say to the marker?

"Draw, pardner!"

What did the plus sign say to the minus sign?

"You are so negative."

What is the capital of Washington?

W.

Bob: What's 5Q plus 5Q?

Todd: TenQ.

Bob: You're welcome!

Gina: I've been swimming since I was five years old.

Gus: You must be tired!

What did Tennessee?

The same thing that Arkansas.

What's a 10-letter word that starts with gas?

Automobile.

Knock, knock.
Who's there?
Hatch.
Hatch who?
Ha, ha. Made you sneeze!

What speaks every language?
An echo.

Knock, knock.
Who's there?
Pencil.
Pencil who?
Your pencil fall down if you don't wear a belt.

Why didn't the quarter roll down the hill with the nickel?

Because it had more cents.

Zachary: Do you want to hear a long joke?
Kayla: Sure.
Zachary: Joooooooooke.

Where do race cars go to wash their clothes?

The laundry vroom.

What would happen if all the cars in the country were painted pink?

It would be a pink car nation.

Why couldn't the bicycle stand up by itself?

It was two tired.

What did the glue say to the piece of paper?

"I'm stuck on you."

Knock, knock.
Who's there?
Cargo.
Cargo who?
Cargo beep, beep.

How is 2 + 2 = 5 like your left foot?

It's not right.

Jessica: What letter does yellow start with?

Paul: Y.

Jessica: Because I want to know!

What did the pencil say to the paper?

"I dot my i's on you."

First scientist: We have discovered that exercise will help kill germs.
Second scientist: But how in the world are we going to get germs to exercise?

What did the pen say to the pencil?

"So, what's your point?"

How do you divide sixteen apples evenly among seventeen people?

Make applesauce.

What is a statue's favorite type of dessert?

Marble cake.

How do you get 27 kids to carve a statue?

Just have everybody chip in.

Why do pandas like old movies?

Because they're in black and white.

What rock group has four men that don't sing?

Mount Rushmore.

What tools do you need to do math?

Multipliers.

What is the world's longest punctuation mark?

The hundred-yard dash.

What is the world's tallest building?

The library, because it has the most stories.

Where do comedians go for lunch?

The laugh-eteria.

What can go through water and not get wet?

Sunlight.

What did the molecule's mom say to him every morning?

"Up and atom!"

What did the nine say to the six?

"Why are you standing on your head?"

What kind of phone does a turtle use?

A shell phone.

Marley: Did you hear what the pirate movie was rated?
Mimi: No, what?
Marley: Arrrrrrrrrgh!

What did the paper clip say to the magnet?

"You're so attractive!"

What do you call a mollusk on a ship?

A snailer.

...21, 22, 23, 24, 25!

Knock, knock.
Who's there?
Radio.
Radio who?
Radio not, here I come.